Made with L[ove]
by Mummy

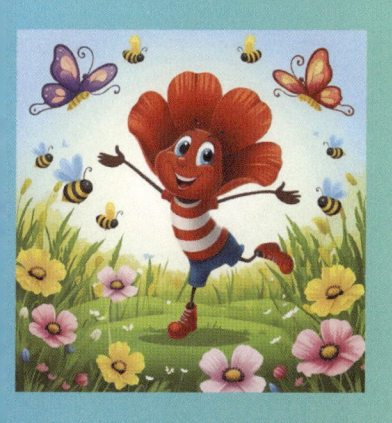

by Poppy Meadows
Look me up for new book releases
instagram.com/poppymeadowsbooks
Copyright 2025

This book belongs to
_____

Mummy had a dream, it's true
She dreamed of someone just like you.

Some families are big, some are small,
But love makes the best family of all!

Mummies and Daddies, two or just one,
Families are love, and love is fun!

Mummy had love and so much to give.
A dream of a baby to cherish and live.

Mummy made a plan, her love so clear,
A trip to the doctor, to bring you near.

Mummy went to see the doctor, to change her life and make it brighter!

Doctor found a seed so bright, planted it with love and light!

I wished and dreamed both day and night.
Grow, sweet baby, warm and tight

One day, the doctor said, 'Hooray! A little baby's on the way!

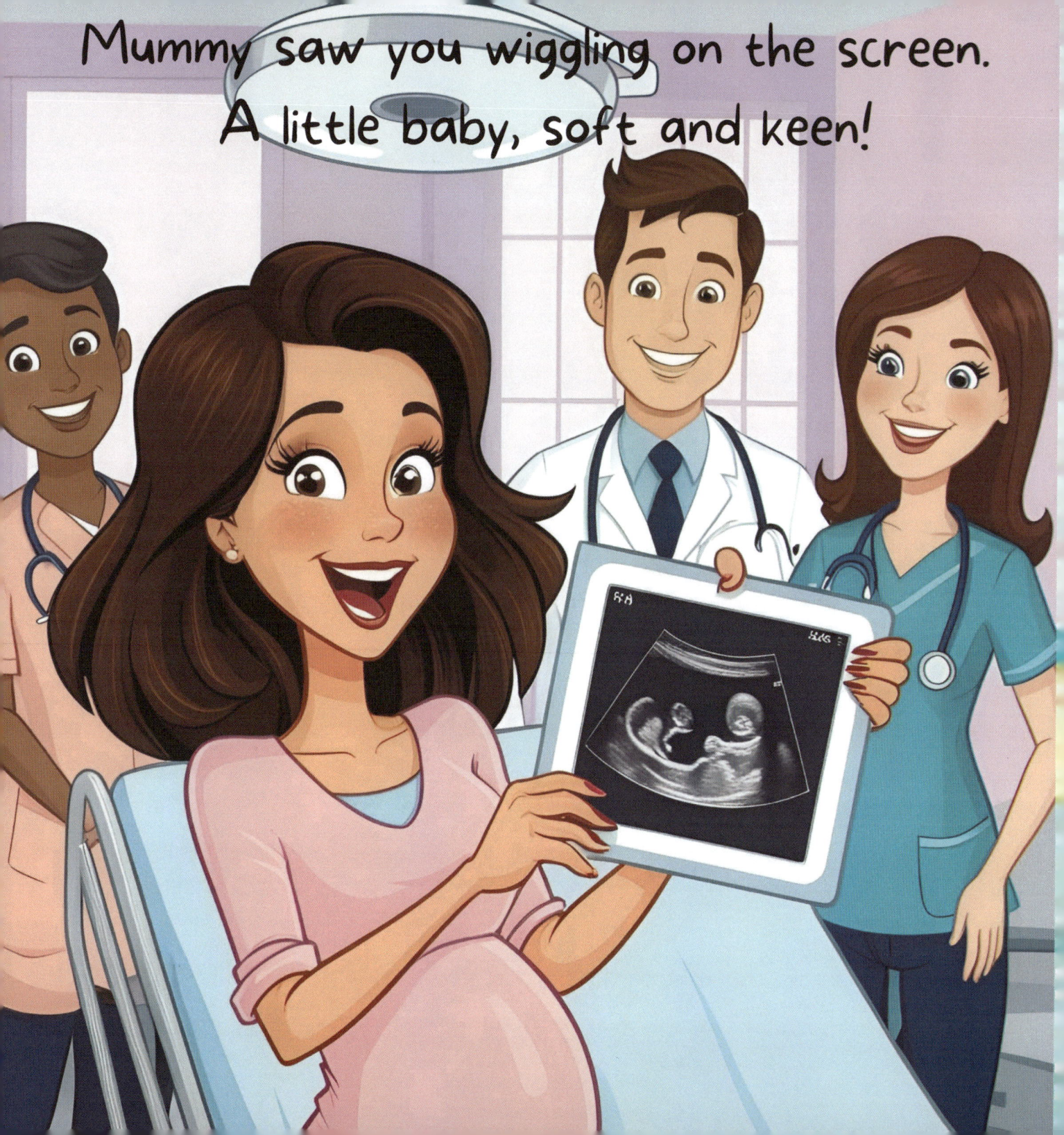

Mummy saw you wiggling on the screen.
A little baby, soft and keen!

Mummy sang and read to you each day, gave you cuddles, kept you safe that way.

A little flutter, soft and new.
Tiny feet that kicked for you!

Toys and blankets, snug and small.
Mummy made a home for all!

It's delivery day, the wait is done,
Soon you'll be here, my little one!

The dream came true.
A baby soft and sweet as you!

Moonlight shone, the stars were bright.
Mummy held you all through the night.

Tiny toes in bubbly streams,
First bath fills the night with dreams.

You are my dream, my heart, my love.
My little gift from stars above.

Giggles, tummy rolls, crawls that flow,
Each day, my love, I watched you grow.

First steps wobble, oh so sweet.
Mummy's there to catch your feet!

And now we laugh, we hug, we play.
Together, always, every day!

You are my joy, my love, my heart.
Together forever, never apart!

However your journey may start.
Family is made with love from the heart.

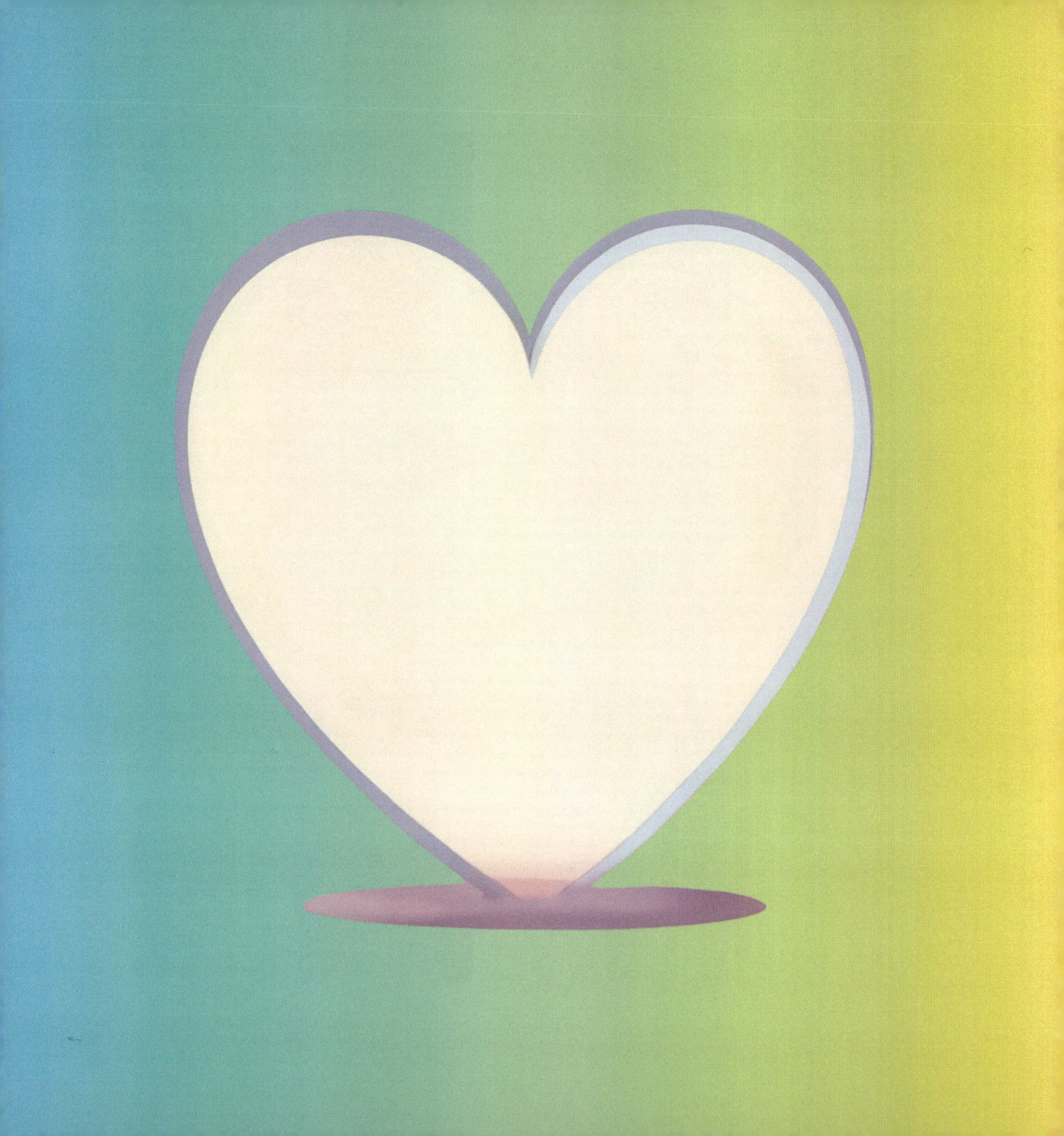

I dedicate this book to my sweet son,
my little miracle,
Your first giggles, your first steps, and every moment in between have painted my world with joy I never knew existed.
This book is for you, my love, a tiny treasure to remember these magical beginnings.
Forever and always,
love Mummy

© 2025 Poppy Meadows. All rights reserved.

Printed in Great Britain
by Amazon